Anthony van Dyck

Alix Wood

**WINDMILL
BOOKS**

New York

Published in 2015 by **Windmill Books**, An Imprint of Rosen Publishing
29 East 21st Street, New York, NY 10010

Copyright © 2015 Alix Wood Books

Adaptations to North American edition © 2015 Windmill Books
An Imprint of Rosen Publishing

Editor for Alix Wood Books: Eloise Macgregor
Designer: Alix Wood

Photo Credits: Cover, 1, 8 © PD-Art; 3, 4 bottom, 14, 25 bottom, 28 © Shutterstock; 4 top
© Uffizi Gallery; 5 top © Boughton House; 5 bottom © Academy of Fine Arts Vienna; 6 ©
Velvet; 7 © Scottish National Gallery; 9, 17, 24 © nga/Andrew W. Mellon Collection; 10, 11,
13, 18 © nga/Widener Collection; 15, 19 © Royal Collection; 16 © National Gallery, London;
20 © Alte Pinakothek; 21 © nga/Samuel H. Kress Collection; 22 top © nga/Rosenwald
Collection; 22 bottom © nga/Arthus and Charlotte Vershbow; 23 © nga/Leo Steinbers; 25
top © Detroit Institute of Arts; 26 © public domain; 27 © Barber Institute of Fine Arts; 29 ©
Huntington Art Gallery, California

Library of Congress Cataloging-in-Publication Data
Wood, Alix.
 Anthony van Dyck / Alix Wood.
    pages cm. — (Artists through the ages)
 Includes index.
ISBN 978-1-4777-5398-9 (pbk.)
ISBN 978-1-4777-5399-6 (6 pack)
ISBN 978-1-6153-3921-1 (library binding)
1. Van Dyck, Anthony, 1599-1641—Juvenile literature. 2. Artists—Belgium—Biography—
Juvenile literature. I. Title.
 N6973.D9W66 2015
 759.9493—dc23
 [B]
                                2014028092

Manufactured in the United States of America

CPSIA Compliance Information: Batch #CW15WM: For Further Information contact Windmill Books, New York, New York at 1-866-478-0556

Contents

Who Was Van Dyck?......................4

Learning and Traveling 6

An Ambitious Man.......................8

Getting a Reputation......................10

Religious Paintings 12

King Charles I................................14

The London Workshop 16

Reflections 18

Settled in England 20

The Etchings..................................22

Mixing Paints..................................24

Watercolors 26

Van Dyck's Last Years....................28

Glossary...30

Websites 31

Read More and Index.....................32

Who Was Van Dyck?

Sir Anthony van Dyck was a **Flemish** artist. He is most famous for being a court painter in England where he painted portraits of King Charles I and his family. He also painted stories from the bible and from myths and legends.

Van Dyck's **self-portrait** painted around 1632

Map of the World

North America

Europe

Asia

Africa

South America

Australia

Van Dyck was born in Antwerp in 1599. Antwerp is in Belgium, in an area known as Flanders.

Antwerp

Young Talent

Van Dyck's wealthy parents sent him to study painting with Hendrick van Balen at the age of 10! Van Dyck became a professional painter when he was around 16 years old. He set up a workshop with his even younger friend Jan Brueghel the Younger.

Portrait of Van Balen by Van Dyck

This self-portrait was painted when Van Dyck was only 15 years old. He already showed a great talent for portraits. His talent was noticed by the well-known artist Sir Peter Paul Rubens, who invited him to his **studio**.

Learning and Traveling

Van Dyck studied for a while with Rubens. Rubens ran a large studio in Antwerp producing paintings for European nobles and art collectors. Van Dyck helped Rubens in his studio. Rubens once said in a letter that Van Dyck was his best pupil.

Rubens designed his Italian-style Antwerp villa and gardens himself. In the next door studio he ran his workshop. His students helped produce much of his work.

Rubens's villa and studio in Antwerp

Learning Printmaking

Van Dyck learned how to make **etchings** and prints at Rubens's studio. Rubens had many talented **engravers** working there. Many of these skilled engravers later worked for Van Dyck.

Van Dyck visited England and then moved to Genoa in Italy. He painted portraits of wealthy **aristocrats** there. He painted full-length portraits similar to the style Rubens had used when he was in Genoa. His paintings were very popular.

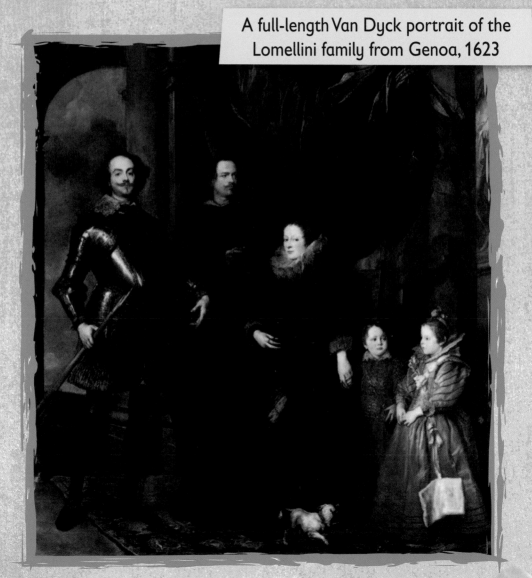

A full-length Van Dyck portrait of the Lomellini family from Genoa, 1623

An Ambitious Man

Van Dyck wanted to be as successful as Rubens. He began to dress in stylish, expensive clothes and employ servants. He dressed more like an aristocrat than an ordinary man. He wore silks, gold chains, and a hat with feathers! While in Genoa he did not mix with other Flemish artists. They thought Van Dyck believed he was better than them.

Self-portrait with a Sunflower, painted after 1633, shows how Van Dyck liked to dress stylishly.

Van Dyck arrived in Italy as a guest of the Balbi family. Gio Agostino Balbi had been a friend of Van Dyck back in Antwerp. He traveled with Van Dyck back to Genoa, but died on the way. Van Dyck brought the sad news of his death to his family.

Portrait of Marchesa Balbi, around 1623

A Guest

Van Dyck gave the Balbi family a portrait of Gio Agostino that he had painted while in Antwerp. Van Dyck stayed as the family's guest for several weeks before setting up his own studio in Genoa. He painted several portraits for the family.

Getting A Reputation

Van Dyck stayed in Italy for six years. He studied paintings by the Italian masters and earned money painting portraits. In Genoa, wealthy families thought having their portrait painted by a famous artist was a **status symbol**.

Filippo Cattaneo, 1623

Van Dyck painted several portraits of aristocratic children. This portrait is of four-year-old Filippo Cattaneo. Although the boy is very young, Van Dyck makes him look quite powerful. With one hand on his hip, and the other hand holding his puppy's chain, Filippo looks like he has a strong character.

Marchesa Elena Grimaldi Cattaneo, 1623

Van Dyck painted Filippo's mother looking very important. A servant holds a **parasol** over her head looking almost like a halo from a religious painting.

To Tall?

Van Dyck often made his portrait subjects look taller than they really were. He did this by viewing them from below and making their limbs look longer.

Religious Paintings

Van Dyck painted several religious paintings when he was in Italy. He worked on paintings for a number of important buildings in the city for local **cardinals** and even for the Pope!

His paintings were influenced by Rubens. He used a similar **composition** and style. Van Dyck did not have as many people in his religious paintings as Rubens did, though. He liked to have one central figure, a little like in his portraits.

The painting opposite is called *The Virgin as Intercessor*. An intercessor is someone who begs for help for another person. The angels flying around hold religious symbols. The wreath of roses may refer to Saint Rosalie, who was a favorite saint of Van Dyck.

Saint Rosalie

Van Dyck belonged to a group that brought holy **relics** of Saint Rosalie from Sicily to Antwerp. It was thought that the relics might protect the town from the **plague**.

King Charles I

King Charles I of England was an eager art collector. He wanted to bring the world's best painters to England. Rubens had visited and was **knighted** for his services. Van Dyck decided to go to England too.

He was given a house on the river and rooms in Eltham Palace. He was knighted, paid a pension, and paid for each painting. The king and queen built a causeway from the river to Van Dyck's studio so that they could visit more easily by boat.

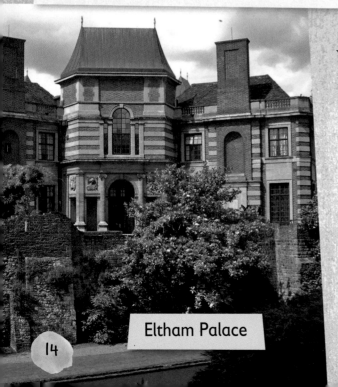

Eltham Palace

Van Dyck painted portraits of the king, the queen, and their children. The portraits were given to supporters of the king. He painted around forty portraits of King Charles and about thirty of the queen.

Three Portraits of a King

Van Dyck's triple portrait of King Charles I was sent to the sculptor, Bernini, in Rome. Bernini used the different angles of the king's face to create a sculpture. The likeness was a success. The king paid Bernini in jewelry worth more than 60 times what the average Roman earned in a year! The sculpture was probably destroyed in a fire in 1698.

The London Workshop

Van Dyck's success meant he needed a workshop in London to keep up with demand! He employed assistants to help him complete his work. The studio became a **production line** for portraits.

Van Dyck would start a portrait by making a drawing on paper. This drawing was enlarged and drawn onto a canvas by an assistant. Van Dyck painted the head himself. The sitters often left the clothes they wanted to wear in the painting at the studio. Other artists often painted the clothes for Van Dyck's portraits.

Lord John Stuart and his brother Lord Bernard Stuart, around 1638

One Hour Each!

Van Dyck never worked for more than one hour on each portrait. Once the hour was up, he would arrange another appointment with that sitter and welcome in the next one. He could work on several portraits in one day in this way.

Philip, Lord Wharton, 1632

Reflections

Van Dyck was very skilled at painting light reflections. You can see the light glinting on the metal in the armor in the painting below and opposite. He was also a master at painting fabric and costumes.

Landscapes

Van Dyck hardly did any landscape paintings. He used landscapes as a background to many of his paintings however. The backgrounds would often be painted by his assistants.

The Prefect Raffaele Raggi, 1625

Charles I with M. de St. Antoine, 1633. Van Dyck often painted King Charles on a horse to make him appear taller. The King was only 5 feet 4 inches (163 cm) tall and was a bit embarrassed about his height.

Settled in England

Van Dyck married Mary Ruthven in 1639. She was one of the queen's ladies-in-waiting, who acted as a personal assistant to the queen. Their marriage may have been a way for the king to try to keep Van Dyck in England.

Van Dyck had become unhappy in England. He made many trips home to Antwerp. He had spent most of 1634 back in Antwerp. He returned there in 1635 and in 1640, too. In 1640 he also traveled with Prince John Casimir of Poland, and painted the prince's portrait.

Mary Ruthven. Van Dyck painted this portrait of his wife between 1635-1640.

The Queen

French princess Henrietta Maria married Charles I when she was just 15 years old.

Queen Henrietta Maria with Sir Jeffrey Hudson, 1634. Jeffrey Hudson was a court dwarf. He had been given to the queen after amusing her one day at a banquet by bursting out of a large pie!

The Etchings

Van Dyck created a series of etchings of portraits of important people of the time. He etched eighteen of the faces himself, but an engraver finished the work. For the rest of the series, Van Dyck drew the portraits on paper and the engravers turned the drawings into plates to print from.

How to Etch

Etchers coat a metal plate with beeswax. Then they draw the design into the wax with a sharp tool. They dip the plate in acid to eat away the areas unprotected by the beeswax. They cover the plate in ink and make a print.

Self-Portrait. Van Dyck drew and then etched the head of his self-portrait. The engraver Jacobus Neeffs then finished the engraving.

Van Dyck's series included portraits of princes, politicians, military men, statesmen, scholars, artists, and art collectors. The portrait below is of the Bishop of Ghent. The bishop had bought some of Van Dyck's paintings for his churches.

Anton Triest, 1632

Mixing Paints

Van Dyck was an expert at mixing colors. In Italy he used rich colors to suit the Italians' tastes, which made his work more popular there. In Antwerp he used a silvery sheen in his portraits so that his subjects were bathed in light. During his time in England, Van Dyck used strong colors and created his own color-mixing **techniques**.

This early portrait of a mother and daughter was painted in Antwerp. The dark background and clothes show up their pale silvery faces. Susanna was related to Rubens's wife. When his wife died, Rubens married Susanna's sister Helena.

Susanna Fourment and Her Daughter, 1621

Van Dyke Brown

Van Dyck often used a deep brown color in his paintings. The paint color "Van Dyke Brown" is named after him. English-speakers often spell his name "Dyke" rather than "Dyck." In the family portrait above, the brown is used in the hair, clothing, and even the greenery in the background. A photography technique that produces rich brown prints is named "Van Dyke Brown," too.

Watercolors

Even though Van Dyck was best known for his oil painting, he also pioneered the use of see-through watercolor washes. The artist left areas of blank paper showing through the paint, which at the time was a new technique.

Avenue in the Country,
around 1637

Watercolor Sketches

Van Dyck sketched watercolor landscapes to use as reference for backgrounds in his other paintings. This sketch of Greenwich in England is a quick, loosely painted impression of the trees and distant ships. You can see the paper showing through.

Van Dyck's Last Years

Charles I was not a popular king. Van Dyck began to realize that Charles's power was fading. He left England and traveled to Antwerp and Paris. He tried to work for the king of Luxembourg, but the king had already hired other artists. Van Dyck went back to Antwerp, and then returned to England.

Back in London, Charles and his family were afraid that there may be a **civil war**. They had no time for portraits. Van Dyck had become ill. The king sent a doctor to look after him, but Van Dyck died at home at the age of 42. His wife had given birth to their daughter, Justina, only eight days before he died.

A statue of Van Dyck in Antwerp, Belgium

Van Dyck was buried in Old Saint Paul's Cathedral, an honor given to the most important British subjects. The king put up a monument to him. It was destroyed in the Great Fire of London in 1666. A plaque to Van Dyck has since been put up in the **crypt** at Saint Paul's.

After Van Dyck

Other things besides paint have been named after Van Dyck. A "Van Dyke beard" is the short, pointed beard worn by many of the men in his portraits. A Cavalier-style costume like the one worn by Thomas Gainsborough's *Blue Boy* (right) was called a "Van Dyke," too. Thomas Gainsborough was one of many artists influenced by Van Dyck's style.

Blue Boy, Thomas Gainsborough, 1770

Glossary

aristocrats
(uh-RIS-tuh-kratz)
The rich and powerful
upper classes.

cardinals (KAHRD-nulz)
High church officials.

civil war
(SIH-vul WOR)
A war between opposing
groups of citizens of the
same country or nation.

composition
(kahm-poh-ZIH-shun)
The manner in which a
painting is put together.

crypt (KRIHPT)
An underground
burial chamber.

engravers
(en-GRAY-verz)
People who cut or carve
letters or designs.

etchings (EH-chingz)
Prints made from an
etched metal plate.

Flemish (FLEH-mish)
Coming from Flanders.

knighted (NY-ted)
To be made a knight.

parasol (PEHR-uh-sol)
An umbrella which protects against the sun.

plague (PLAYG)
A serious disease causing a high rate of death.

production line (pruh-DUK-shun LYN)
Where a product passes through several stages like in a factory.

relics (REH-liks)
Objects connected with a saint or martyr.

self-portrait (self–POR-tret)
Portrait of oneself made by oneself.

status symbol (STAA-tuhs SIHM-buhl)
A possession that indicates a person's wealth

studio (STOO-dee-oh)
The working place of an artist.

techniques (tek-NEEKS)
Methods of achieving a desired aim.

Websites

For web resources related to the subject of this book, go to: **www.windmillbooks.com/weblinks** and select this book's title.

Read More

Courtauld, Sarah. *Art Sticker Book* (Usborne Sticker Books).
London: Usborne Publishing Ltd., 2009.

Roundhill, Clare. *Portraits* (Artists Workshop). London:
A & C Black Publishers Ltd., 1996.

Index

A

Anton Triest 23

Avenue in the Country
26

B

Balbi family 9

Balen, Hendrick van
5

Blue Boy, 29

C

Charles I, King 4, 14,
15, 19, 28

Charles I with M. de St
Antoine 19

G

Gainsborough, Thomas
29

L

Lomellini family 7

Lord John Stuart and
his brother Lord
Bernard Stuart 16

M

Marchesa Elena
Grimaldi Cattaneo,
11

Mary Ruthven 20

P

Philip, Lord Wharton
17

Portrait of Marchesa
Balbi 9

Prefect Raffaele Raggi,
The 18

Q

Queen Henrietta
Maria with Sir Jeffrey
Hudson 21

R

Rubens, Sir Peter Paul
5, 6, 7, 8, 12, 14

S

Self-portraits 4, 5, 22

Self-Portrait with a
Sunflower 8

Susanna Fourment and
Her Daughter 24

V

Virgin as Intercessor,
The 12-13